fowl play

For Hamish

First published in 2005 by New Holland Publishers (NZ) Ltd
Auckland • Sydney • London • Cape Town

218 Lake Road, Northcote, Auckland, New Zealand
14 Aquatic Drive, Frenchs Forest, NSW 2086, Australia
86-88 Edgware Road, London, W2 2EA, United Kingdom
80 McKenzie Street, Cape Town 8001, South Africa

www.newhollandpublishers.co.nz

ISBN: 1 86966 094 3

Packaged for New Holland Publishers in 2005 by
 Renaissance Publishing, Auckland
Design: Trevor Newman

A catalogue record for this book is available from the National
Library of New Zealand

10 9 8 7 6 5 4 3 2 1

Colour reproduction by SC (Sang Choy) International Pte Ltd,
 Singapore
Printed in China through Phoenix Offset, Hong Kong

fowl play

DON DONOVAN

NH
NEW
HOLLAND

My father told me
all about the birds
and the bees,
the liar – I went
steady with a
woodpecker till
I was 21.

BOB HOPE

I don't exercise at all.
If God meant us to touch our
toes, he would have put them
further up our body.

ANONYMOUS

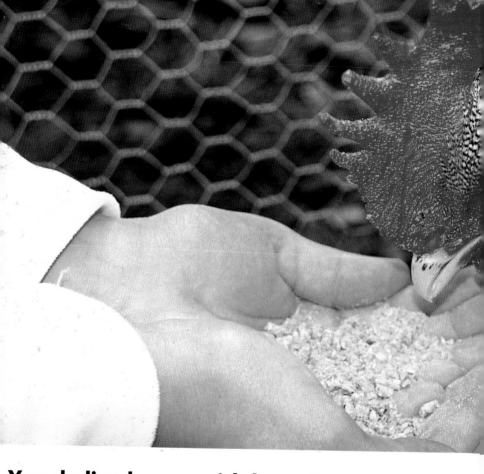

You do live longer with bran, but you spend

the last 15 years on the toilet. ALAN KING

All you need is love.

JOHN LENNON, PAUL McCARTNEY

I've been rich and
I've been poor;
rich is better.

SOPHIE TUCKER

It isn't pollution that's harming the environment. It's the impurities in our air and water that are doing it.

DAN QUAYLE

Do you wake up in the morning feeling sleepy and grumpy? Then you must be Snow White.

DAVID FROST

I'm all in favour of free expression provided it's kept rigidly under control.

ALAN BENNETT

A baby is God's opinion that life should go on.

CARL SANDBURG

It's erotic if you're using a feather. It's kinky if you're using the whole damn chicken.

ANONYMOUS

**Condoms aren't completely safe.
A friend of mine was wearing
one and got hit by a bus.**

BOB RUBIN

Don't be afraid to take a big step. You can't cross a chasm in two small jumps.

DAVID LLOYD GEORGE

OPEN
PARKING

A chicken crossing the road is poultry in motion.

ANONYMOUS

I hate to spread rumours – but what

else can one do with them. AMANDA LEAR

Don't overestimate the decency of the human race.

H.L. MENCKEN

If you don't know where you're going, you'll probably end up somewhere else.

YOGI BERRA

It is not only fine feathers that make fine birds.

AESOP

Do incubator chicks
love their mother?

ARTHUR BAER

Telling a teenager the facts of life is like giving a fish a bath.

ARNOLD H. GLASGOW

Be good and you will be lonely.

MARK TWAIN

I don't do drugs any more 'cause
I find I get the same effect just
by standing up really fast.

JOHNATHAN KATZ

**Have children while
your parents are still
young enough to take
care of them.**

RITA RUDNER

I had a dream last night, I was eating a 10-pound marshmallow. I woke up this morning and the pillow was gone.

TOMMY COOPER

If you're being chased by a police dog, try not to go through a tunnel, then on to a little seesaw, then jump through a hoop of fire. They're trained for that!

MILTON JONES

**Don't count your chickens
before they cross the road.**

ANONYMOUS

Good girls go to heaven, but bad girls get to go everywhere.

HELEN GURLEY BROWN

Never underestimate the power of very

stupid people in large groups. JOHN KENNETH GALBRAITH

The average person thinks he isn't.

REVEREND LARRY LORENZONI

**God made me on a morning
when he had nothing else to do.**

C.F. LLOYD

Vive la difference.

FRENCH PROVERB

When chickens quit quarrelling over their food they often find that there is enough for all of them. I wonder if it might not be the same with the human race.

DON MARQUIS

In real life, I assure you, there is no such thing as algebra.

FRAN LEBOWITZ

We have never understood the fear of some parents about babies getting mixed up in the hospital. What difference does it make if you get a good one?

HEYWOOD BROUN

Good taste is better than bad taste but bad taste is better than no taste.

ARNOLD BENNETT

Most children threaten at times to run away from home. This is the only thing that keeps some parents going.

PHYLLIS DILLER

Whoever thought up the word 'mammogram'? Every time I hear it, I think I'm supposed to put my breast in an envelope and send it to someone.

JAN KING

**When children are doing nothing,
they are doing mischief.**

HENRY FIELDING

Sometimes I'm so sweet even I can't stand it.

JULIE ANDREWS

If this raised a laugh, then try these
other titles by Don Donovan

Chewing the Cud   1 86966 068 4
Pig Tales   1 86966 095 1
Woolly Wisdom   1 86966 063 3